eCommerce
The beginners guide to opening an online shop

Taryn Lee Johnston

copyright FCM Media

Copy Editing by FCM Editing

Cover Design by FCM Media

www.fcmmedia.co.uk

IBSN 978-1494282370

Published by

FCM PUBLISHING

www.fcmpublishing.co.uk

First printed in the UK - December 2013

All rights reserved. No part of this publication may be reproduced

(other than purposes of review) without written consent of the publisher.

Contents

Introduction

5

Starting Points

13

Great Website

33

Converting Strangers into Repeat Customers

47

Social Media Do's & Don'ts

51

Summary

59

Introduction

Selling online isn't easy.

That believe it or not, is GOOD news for you. It means that the market is less saturated at the successful end of the spectrum. Meaning that the more effort you put in and the further along the spectrum you get the more successful your enterprise will be.

Consumer habits have changed dramatically. By 2020, some experts predict that 90 per cent of transactions will take place online or be internet-influenced. If you want your product to be seen and ultimately make you a living it is essential to get on to the global High Street that the internet provides. Many businesses have long used their websites to generate additional revenue, yet in recent years there has also been significant growth in businesses that start up exclusively online.

An online business provides you with a flexible working environment, relatively less risk, significantly less start up costs, access to free marketing in the shape of social media and impulse clicking.

Make no mistake though, this business model does not require any less effort to make it into a successful enterprise.

"The real secret to online success is actually based on very old truths:

Success demands effort, patience and perseverance."

The Primary reason making an online business so desirable is that you don't need the large amount of start up capital that you would with an offline business. What you need is time to invest and a desire to succeed.

Launching a new website can feel like a very unrewarding task. You are working hard on your content, marketing your site across the internet, but your website traffic is hardly improving on a week to week basis. It can be demoralising. However this is normal! Links to your website gain value with age. It takes a while for you to build up your content to a reasonable level where your site can take on a "resource"-like status (so people will come back to it, see what's new, recommend it and talk about it on their blogs).

It is a leap of faith in the beginning, because your efforts often have no immediate effect.

You need to go into the project knowing that it may take several months to build your online presence. It is crucially important to remember this point because so many new website owners give up in the early stages thinking they've "failed" or just lose interest because nothing is happening. This in turn guarantees failure.

Incubation periods for websites can differ depending on the market you are targeting. Expect the period to be longer in more saturated markets and use this time to look at what your competitors are doing. With an online business it is so easy to be your own mystery shopper.

The Incubation period of your website is the first few months after going live when the search engines aren't quite letting you in and your are languishing in the low rankings of search engine results, despite your continued efforts. This is enough to test the most patience of even the most experienced website owner. Do not give up there are millions of people making a living and even becoming millionaires from their online businesses. We hope that this book will give you the first steps to becoming one of those success stories

To paraphrase Winston Churchill :

"When you're going through (Search Engine) hell, keep going".

Starting Points

Setting up a website and selling online has become so accessible that every Tom, Dick and Harriet is doing it, but actually capturing and maintaining a regular and continuous volume of actual sales requires some careful planning and perseverance.

As with any small business, the first step is to conduct market research.

Market Research

Identify your target market

it is essential that you know who you are selling to, give your ideal customer a name and create a back story for why they would buy your product

Identify the places where customers will find you

Once you have identified your core customer, you need to know what they read, where they go, what websites they use, which blogs they read etc. etc. This will give you a clue as to where to concentrate your marketing efforts

Assess demand

You and your mum think this is a great product, but what about the rest of the world? It is never too late to change your product line or to add to it.

Assess your competition

Look at the websites of your competition, follow the breadcrumbs and find out where they place their marketing efforts and watch their social media to find out how they interact within the marketplace.

Set prices that are consistent with your place in the market

It is worth bearing mind that prices that are too low will deter customers just as much as those which are too high.

You will also need to produce a business plan.

If sales are likely to exceed the annual threshold (currently £79,000), you must become VAT-registered. You will also need to pay tax, in accordance with your status as a sole trader or limited company. Online traders must also observe data protection legislation when storing important information about customers. But we will come back to that.

As I have mentioned before, selling online isn't easy, but that difficulty actually helps you to gain a competitive advantage over your rivals.

During the course of this book, you will find out how to maximise the number of visitors to your website and also how to convert those visits into actual 'take to the bank' sales - some tips involve investment of money (i.e advertising space & directories) - many others involve the use of your time and effort.

We will also try to avoid the traditional 'blood, sweat and tears'!

The Keys to online success

Teach Yourself (Google and YouTube are your friends)

Self-teaching is perhaps THE best habit you can get into. The alternative is to treat knowledge as something you can only get from someone else (training course) and this way of thinking always gives you a way out, with excuses such as not having the time and/or it's too expensive. With the internet, now you can learn what you need to know almost immediately. There is always a free alternative online for whatever you want to learn. Join Forums and don't be afraid to ask for help or guidance if you get stuck. You will find that successful people are almost always willing to share their tips for free.

Be Different from Your Competitors

Many companies are selling online successfully without really doing anything different to their competitors. They have most likely established themselves in their market so they simply become a known brand, or are spending a lot of advertising money to aid online sales. It is entirely possible to make a good living selling online without really distinguishing yourself from your competitors.

However, if you're a small business/start-up, you should not take anything for granted. Many start up companies have little confidence and so copy the style and substance of their competitors.

Deliberately NOT being unique is like a race to the bottom. Create something that distinguishes your products/services from your competition.

Unique selling points can include

Being an enthusiast! It helps to love what you do/sell. Not truly being enthusiastic about what you sell (not BELIEVING in what you sell) creates a flat sales pitch and lifeless content on your website.

Offering better value than your competitors (don't just say this on your site - prove it by making price comparisons).

Offering a more comprehensive range of products for sale than your competitors.

Offering a superior service/better quality goods than your competitors.

Offering a better customer service/after-sales care than your competitors. Diving deeper than your competitors: offering more information than them - news, opinion, advice etc.

Be THE resource website for your market; offer unique information that isn't available elsewhere.

By distinguishing yourself in some way, visitors are far more likely to remember you and come back to your website, as well as recommending you to others.

Sales speak ('unbeatable value', 'the best X available') tells your visitors nothing useful, since most of your competitors will also use this jargon. Make your site modern and current by avoiding these clichés. You need to compel visitors into making a sale with simple facts - give visitors clear and simple reasons why they should buy your products. Give a sales pitch in plain English, which is much more powerful than blunted and worn-out phrases.

More observant visitors will also be put off by spelling, grammar and punctuation mistakes.

Visit your competitor's websites on a regular basis to see how they are selling online - find out about their prices, services etc. By learning about your competition, you can learn how to distinguish yourself from them. There is nothing wrong or unethical about checking out the competition.

Manage/Display your product categories & content to aid your visitors AND search engines

Your product/services category listings are the heart of the navigation of your site - this navigation guides your visitors to your products. If your category names are vague, you will confuse your customers - keep them explicit and clear. Take time to research key phrases that are relevant to your market and try to build these key phrases into your product category names. For example, if you're selling sports accessories and you sell footwear, don't just call your category 'footwear' - be specific and call the category 'football boots' as this is a much more useful search term for your users AND for search engines when they index your website.

If this category is broken down into sub-categories, such as ladies or men's boots, call each sub-category specifically 'ladies football boots' and 'mens football boots'. This might seem like a redundant use of the term 'football boots' but it actually helps you GREATLY in getting good ranking positions for the search term 'football boots' as well as 'ladies football boots' and 'mens football boots'.

Having said that, don't create too many categories as this can be just as confusing as too few, even if you are selling a wide variety of products. Too many categories and your site suddenly becomes much more difficult for your visitor to browse. Keep your main categories down to 10 or less. You can always break these main categories down into sub- and sub-sub categories. Search engines will follow all these categories, so your sub-categories will also be indexed.

Product names, photos, and product descriptions

Make your product names clear and to the point -

don't call them by an obscure product code, unless that product code happens to be well known in your market and a useful search term.

Again, try to include a useful search term in the product name. For example, if I'm selling Nike Football Boots, I might use the product name "Nike Mercurial Vapour FG Football Boot" just to include the full product name as well as the basic category name it belongs to. It's explicit while including an extra instance of the key phrase 'football boot'.

Make sure you have hi-res, clear photos of the products that you are selling. Photograph them from different angles, and try to include 3 or 4 images per product. This helps your visitor 'weigh up' the product and makes it much more tangible.

Poor photos are guaranteed to make your site look amateur and reduce the likelihood of turning the visit into a sale.

Mention the product name often in the description without it sounding unnatural. This helps with your key phrase density (your product detail page should be optimised to the product name). Keep descriptions detailed and interesting; the description is your sales pitch - it's also more content to be indexed onto search engines. Don't just copy and paste some sales literature - keep it fresh and original, and therefore useful for your visitors.

Keep your site up-to-date to attract repeat visitors, commit time and effort to your site

Give your visitors a reason to bookmark your site - keep adding new content - start a blog about the industry you're in; write articles telling your visitors new useful ways your product/services can be used. Search engines also like websites that are constantly updated and favour them.

Imagine walking along the high street, if a shop never changed it's window display or added new items to it's stock would you bother to go in? Your online shop is the same. Make it interesting and current.

Take the time to get product reviews even if you and your family are the ones testing them. Customers like to know how something works or how it's going to improve their life - make your products necessary!

Pricing Levels

When selling online, your item prices should be set to 'optimal' to maximise sales; this value isn't always apparent until experimenting with the price of each item.

Your visitors may like your items and be convinced by your promises of service and trust your company, but the price may prevent them from buying.

Create special offers - putting items/categories on short special offers to learn where these optimal prices can be found.

Sometimes prices can be too low and visitors view your site suspiciously!

Again check out your competition, don't deliberately undercut but make sure you're in the right pricing league.

Remember

"Everyone Loves a Bargain, but no one likes cheap"

Build trust

People visiting your site are looking for signs of trustworthiness - a lack of trust is guaranteed not to get you a sale.

One tip to get your visitors to trust you is to have a nice big telephone number on the top header part of your web-page, that features throughout the site. Let people know your 'open hours' for the phone too - they won't expect you to be 24/7 if you're a small business. It means there's somebody physically running this site - someone to talk to at the very least. It's also good for your sales as you're more likely to convince somebody by talking to them than you are by text on your webpages.

Reassure your visitors - give them a money-back guarantee if possible. Write your terms and conditions in plain English and keep them to an absolute minimum - see how few words you can write your terms and conditions in.

Get trusted websites to link to your

website

Search engines like trusted websites - they want their results to be sure and reliable and hate sites with no track record of trust. You can get your own 'trust track record' by creating original content that is constantly kept up-to-date. This will give your site more value in the eyes of other website owners who are far more likely to link to you - these should be website owners who also have original, fresh content.

Guest posts. Write informative and unique articles on other websites and get a clean, branded link back to your site via the "bio" box. Even in these post-Penguin days, you will be safe with these kinds of links so long as they are from sites relevant to your own and have some degree of authority.

Contribute on forums. Joining a forum and contributing to it helps build trust. Pick forums in your website's niche and help other forum members with their questions/queries. And of course, don't be shy with placing links to your website in the posts you make on the forum - all good if you're seen as a trusted forum member.

Whatever you do, avoid begging for links by emailing companies. It's proven to give you a poor return for the amount of time you spend. It also annoys companies who receive the unsolicited email.

Commit time and effort to your site, the more you give it the more you'll receive. At the beginning of your business you have the time to dedicate, as you get busier you'll find it harder so put in place right now things that will make your life easier and get into habits that will in the long run save you time - like setting aside 1 day a month for admin & accounting work.

Great

Website

Having a great looking website is only half the battle but it is a very large and important half. If your site is not attractive customers will not be enticed to stay and look around. If your site does look professional, your prospective clients will assume that you are not professional and click away quicker than you can say 'drop and drag'.

Identify the purpose of your site. What you want isn't always what you need and that impressively creative interface of your dreams will probably only hinder navigation around your site or overshadow your product.

Why are you launching this new website? What is your end goal? As obvious as that sounds, ask yourself that question on a daily basis as new trends, technology and products may have a bearing on the answer.

Getting your site up and running

You must decide whether to create your own business website or get someone else to do it for you. Doing it yourself can save money, but the results may not be as professional as you would want.

There are many ready-made online solutions that allow people with little experience to create their own website. However, you might prefer to pay a professional website designer. This should give better results, and will cost around £500-£800. Setting a budget and clear brief will help you to minimise the costs.

Many people start out asking the wrong questions

Can you make my site look like such and such a website? That's a common question I get when I get an enquiry for a website. Usually it's simply that they like the layout or scheme of the site but it doesn't always match the purpose of their site.

Here's a conversation I've had a few times

Enquirer: "We need our site to look like {insert big brand name website}. We need decent rankings in the search engine, and we have no budget for advertising the site. We want the site to be easy to use."

Me {visits website} : "There is a problem as that site is entirely developed in Flash. This means your site will be difficult to use for a good number of your visitors (those with particular disabilities, those using an iPhone and some other mobile devices, etc), Flash is not really very visible to search engines.

Enquirer : "well, the brand is obviously famous, they're doing well, they chose this type of site, so it's something I want to for my own site."

Me : "They can afford to not care about the issues I've mentioned as they are already very successful in the market, you need to care about these issues because you are a start-up and you will need every advantage you can get over your competitors to succeed."

Enquirer : "I understand what you're saying, BUT I need it to look like this site"

And so it continues. The enquirer's business goals are being jeopardised by the enquirer himself putting obstacles in the way.

Optimal design is the only way to make your business stand out and work for you.

It's not just Flash though. There are many other ways to sabotage your own site before it's even built! Some people want graphical icon navigation (without text) - so you have to guess what each icon represents, Drop down menus that only appear on rollover, audio/video that will auto play when a page loads and popup windows etc.

Your website is like a car that must take you from A to B everyday without fail. A website must help facilitate your principle goal - which is sales, and not hinder it in anyway.

The correct marketing will largely determine the success of your website and search engine optimisation (SEO) is crucial to this. At ground level, it means using words within your website that ensure a high placing on search engine (eg Google) results pages. You could also use paid for advertising services such as Google Adwords, which are charged on a pay-per-click basis.

Website information you must include

- Your address and contact details
- Privacy policy
- Terms and conditions
- Exchange and refund policy
- Quality commitment
- Information about delivery and payment.

Stock availability and pricing should be kept up to date and you must always state how much VAT and P&P is payable per item.

To collect payments you will need to include a shopping cart function, as well as a secure means by which customers can enter their card details when paying. Most website designers provide a shopping cart function and payment facility as part of their service. Online website building packages will also provide them.

A suitable merchant account is also needed to collect payments. Providers such as PayPal are popular, but you should also enquire at your bank. All merchant accounts will charge a service charge on each transaction a set up fee as well as a monthly service fee. So do shop around and compare all of the options for the one that best suits your business.

Test and protect your website

Be sure to test your website site thoroughly before you launch. Ask potential customers as well as your mother what they think. Put your pride on the back seat and react to all feedback wether it be good or bad.

"Running an online business isn't without risk. Serious technical or security issues can have a disastrous consequence, so make sure you protect your website from online threats and back up important data."

In a Nutshell

- Establish your strategy

Will the online side of your business be used for selling goods and services, generating sales leads and displaying your product range, or for providing post sales support? You'll need to work out every stage of a transaction before pushing ahead - buying from other e-commerce sites will tell you what works well, and what doesn't.

- Build your online shop

Your website will often be the first point of contact with customers, so it must project the right image of your business. In particular, customers should be able to view your offer and buy without difficulty. But you should also think also about security, delivery, customers contact, keeping it updated and compliance with distance selling regulations.

- Choose an online payment system

You can take money for goods bought online in a variety of ways. Most companies set up a payment facility with their bank and/or use an established online payment service such as PayPal. Both have a small cost per transaction, but make buying straightforward and hassle free.

- Get it right behind the scenes

The way in which you handle orders has a major impact on customer perception and a trouble-free journey from purchase to receipt of goods can turn a one-off sale into repeat business. An automated system can deliver speed and efficiency to the order process and link up the different people in your company who might be handling the order.

- Deliver the goods

Choose which distribution channels to use to get the goods to customers. In the case of software, for instance, delivery could be via downloads; send physical items via the postal service or private couriers. Consider offering an express delivery service and enable customers to track their order. Fast, safe delivery creates a good impression - as does a transparent returns policy.

- Market your online outlet

It's no use having a great online sales channel if no one knows about it. Internet marketing, such as search engine optimisation, pay-per-click advertising and an e-newsletter, will get potential customers to your site. Free software from search engines will help you get more information about what visitors respond to, so you can refine your marketing further.

- Know the regulations

If you sell online, you have to follow a number of laws and regulations to ensure you trade fairly, including the Data Protection Act 1998, the Electronic Commerce Regulations 2002, and the Consumer Protection (Distance Selling) Regulations 2000. These ensure that personal data provided by customers is kept secure, goods and services meet quality and suitability standards, and online contracts are legally binding.

- Be secure

It's important to protect against people hacking into your data. Virus software, password protection and firewalls offer front line protection. Other contingency measures such as having a back-up site available are also an option.

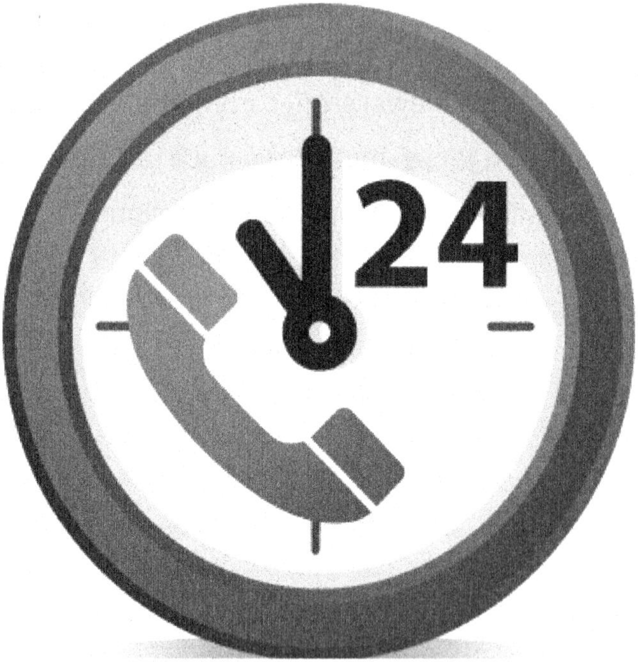
24

Converting Strangers to Repeat Customers

There are 5 basic steps to converting a complete stranger into a repeat customer

1. Effective Marketing - which brings visitors to your website
2. Quality Content - your marketing works, and you've got an audience. Now you need to give a good first impression: do they like what you're selling? are they buying at your price point? Is your presentation easy to navigate? Does your content reflect your product and your business in the best way?
3. Strong Trust Factor - Your marketing has worked and you have web traffic, market research says people like your products and prices, but they need to trust you now before buying anything.
4. Usability - they found you, they like your products, they trust you, now how easy is it to actually buy?

5. Taking Care of Your Customers - they found you, they liked your products, they trust you, they could easily buy your products. Now can you get them to buy again? Repeat business is a wonderful thing. It's a lot easier to keep a customer than trying to constantly find new ones.

Without marketing, nobody finds your website, so points 2,3,4 and 5 are irrelevant.

Without the right products/services/prices, nobody wants to buy your products so points 3,4 and 5 are irrelevant.

Without winning the trust of your visitors, points 4 and 5 are irrelevant.

On point 4, a difficult checkout process means you will lose many potential customers - many potential REPEAT customers.

Succeeding at all 5 points will maximise your sales conversions and actually make running your business a lot easier

Simple advice, but in the age of the slogan 'work smarter, not harder', it's often over-looked: persevere with your website. It will not be an instant success. The quietest, most unsuccessful time will almost certainly be the first few months of your site's existence. A horrible misconception is that everything is magically automated online, including making money. It isn't.

Social Media Do's & Don'ts

As with all business decisions take time to review the different platforms, get to know them and how they would represent your business. Don't rush in joining as many as you can in one hit as many of them will be either too time consuming to maintain or not relevant for your business.

Whilst the scattergun approach may get your website seen in many different places it's unlikely you'll have the time or inclination to keep them up to date once your initial spurt of enthusiasm has worn off.

The obvious candidates are Twitter, Facebook, LinkedIn, YouTube, Myspace and Google+ of course you can then branch out and look at more niche marketing sites but initially these are the sites best placed to get you started.

"So do I need all of them? - No is the simple answer."

The popular consensus is that every business should have a Twitter and a LinkedIn account as the bare minimum. These are both at the "business" end of the spectrum and allow you to network socially and promote your business to the people that are interested in hearing from you.

Many businesses are simply not suited to Facebook, and having a static page with no "Likes" or content can potentially be more damaging than not having one at all. A site that isn't updated or current can give the impression that a company is no longer trading or, even worse, just doesn't care.

Does it have to take all day everyday and will you still have time to actually work? Well, unless you're me (I professionally manage other peoples social media accounts) then no you shouldn't be on social media sites all day! There are a couple of 'good practice' rules to get into and then it's down to you to invest as much time as you realistically can afford.

As I mentioned earlier though it is important that you don't allow your sites to become dormant, try to do something every day so that people begin to get to know you, remember you and ultimately send you money!

Best practice

- Use Management Tools.

I recommend Hootsuite but there are others such as Tweetdeck and Seesmic. This means you only have to say it once which saves you valuable time.

- Post on the move.

Most of us have a phone that can connect to the internet, so use this. If you're out and see something worthwhile then share it. Please do bear in mind, however that most people do not want to see a picture of your lunch.

- Set aside 1 day a month.

Use this time to schedule business tweets, write your blog and update your website. Once that's done you can then use any other time for sociable posts that allow potential customers to see you as a real person. Remember people buy from people not companies.

- Acknowledge.

If someone takes the time to comment, mention or Re-Tweet you then acknowledge it. Get in the habit of being friendly and good mannered.

- Know when to promote yourself

Yes I know that sounds like a contradiction but nothing will lose you followers as quickly as a tweet like this "Thanks for the RT if you need new windows/SEO/loft insulation click here.."

- Do not Tell us you're in a coffee shop

Unless of course there's a brand new flavour, great discount or any other reason for us to visit. The same applies for buying fish fingers in Tesco the only people that really want that information are Birds Eye and Tesco!

"Social media is here to stay and is an invaluable tool for any business especially small businesses that have little or no marketing budget. All of these sites are free to use and the only cost is your time. Can you afford not to?"

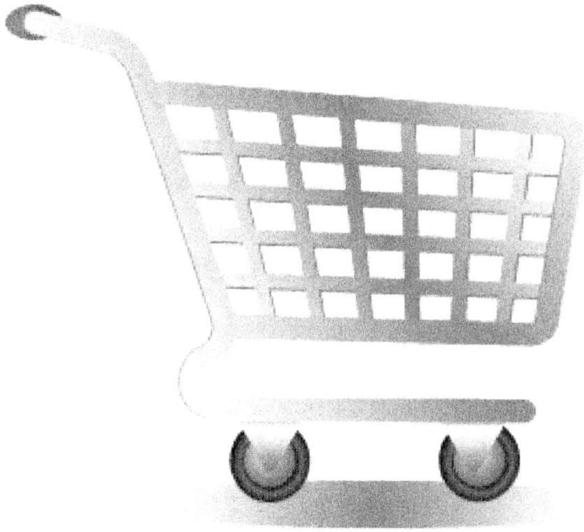

Summary

Top 10 Online Selling Tips

So here it is.. If you are the sort of person who only reads the last chapter of a book, you are in luck because this one is a good one.

1. Having a website is a must for all professional businesses.

Customers expect that all legitimate businesses have websites. Having a website helps businesses convey their value and sell their products and services even when the owner is sleeping.

2. Analyse your competition to maximise your position in the market.

It's obvious, but very few business owners actually analyse their competition properly. When you understand your competition, you know how position your likeness and your uniqueness.

Both are important, especially when competing against larger companies.

3. Sell through all available 'sales channels'.

There are two main categories of sales channel: direct sales, where you sell directly to the customer, and indirect sales, where you have 3rd party businesses buying from you and then selling to their customers. A myriad of direct sales channels are available to you and you should utilise them all. You may choose to sell directly from your website, or through online auction services such as eBay and Amazon.

Don't limit yourself to only one channel - the more channels you have the better your sales figures will be. What about indirect sales channels? Have you considered recruiting a 3rd party to sell or recommend your products and services? Set out and financial reward or commission clearly before you start.

"Once you have all your sales channels working correctly, do not sit back on your bottom line - Go and find more."

4. Convey customer benefits and/or problems solved.

When customers buy your products and services, they do so because what you are offering benefits them or solves their problems. And that knowledge should be the basis for all of your marketing.

5. Use electronic marketing.

Internet marketing and opt-in e-mail newsletters are both important marketing streams to leverage. Internet marketing includes sponsoring keyword searches through search engines and exchanging advertising banners with other related businesses.

Opt-in email newsletters provide a powerful communication method for maintaining customer relationships and increasing sales. These opt-in newsletters provide a friendly reminder of your company, products, and services. You can also reward your customers with vouchers and special offers. Once you have added an opt-in newsletter to your website, you should see a in traffic and sales every time you send a newsletter.

Avoid sending unsolicited e-mail (known as spam). Laws vary by country, but most people despise spam. To protect your business, define your solicitation policy and make it obvious how to opt out of your newsletter.

6. Use phrases throughout your website to which potential buyers will relate.

Use phrases that customers understand throughout your website. This is because after you notify search engines that you have a website, they will add your description to their index. If what you report doesn't match what they find on your website, they will penalise your website position in their index or not index your site at all. Using the most descriptive terms and phrases on your website will help your search

64

engine position.

For example, if you have 'handmade leather handbags' then you will want to add that phrase to your title page, throughout your website pages, and inside your website page links. That way, your site is optimised and ready to be indexed.

7. Notify the top search engines that you exist.

Most search engines such as Google, Yahoo and MSN let you notify them that you have a website. Most offer this as a free service. Make sure that you take advantage of this free service. They will then add your site to their search results, if your website meets their criteria. Be aware that it can take between one to four months to be added.

8. Be consistent.

Be consistent across all of your website pages in how you describe products and services. Also be consistent in you present your brand. Consistency includes layout, word phrases, capitalisation, colours and images. Choose a website template and stick with it throughout your site.

While every site owner wants to be creative, but do note that repetition is often comforting to the customer and allows for brand recognition. Brand recognition is the trigger that builds trust in your customers.

9. Secure information.

If you are selling products and services online, you need to protect your customers' data. Add secure payment processing and a shopping cart to your website. That way, sensitive customer transaction information will be protected and secured. Never send sensitive customer information such as credit card numbers via email. Email is not as secure as you would think.

10. Find a trusted advisor to help you navigate the Internet.

You may know your business inside and out. However, when navigating what need to be done in the digital world, you may feel lost. If you need help building a website, marketing it, or increasing your sales, then seek out advice and help, so that you can get on with building your business.

Common Mistakes

- Requiring Login to Order

Registration is very time consuming, especially when you have yet to establish any relationship with a retailer, and you have no idea if you'll ever purchase again.

- Not Showing Shipping Prices Upfront

In my opinion, the best practice is to simply base your shipping costs on the merchandise total. It might not be the most accurate way, but if you average it out, it works fine.

- Vague, Hard to Find Return Policies

Wherever I can, I like to use the words "No Hassle Return Policy" to reassure the customer that the process is quick and easy.

- Poor SEO

Build it, and they will **not** come, unless your eCommerce site is on good terms with Google.

- Poor Product Descriptions

Your product descriptions are the closest thing you have to an face to face salesperson.

- Lack of Filtering & Sorting

What will your customer need in order to narrow down their options and make a purchase?

- Hard to Find Checkout Button

Imagine not being able to find the checkout lane at a grocery store. Many online stores assume shoppers know that the shopping cart is the first step of the checkout process. To prevent confusion of your customers, always have a clear "checkout" button visible on every page.

- Poor Merchandising

If you owned a real world store, I'm going to bet you would walk your aisles every day making sure that your products are presented properly and that their are no stock issues. Website owners often expect their online stores to run themselves, and rarely take time for this important audit.

- Getting too Personal

Do you really need your customer's date of birth to complete an order? Even asking for information such as email or telephone number may arouse suspicion in your customers.

- No Calls to Action

Don't assume that your visitors will click on image maps or links. Make your call to action buttons big, bold, and clear in your message. Every page of the conversion funnel (landing page to product page to checkout) should clearly define the next step in the process.

Ask yourself an important question for each additional form field you add, "Is this worth losing a sale over?"

- No Error Reporting

From a technical point of view, it's very simple to setup error notifications when certain unexpected events occur on your website. Montastic offers a completely free website monitoring service. In addition, ask your webmaster to setup email alerts for every time a 500 (internal server) error or 404 (page not found) error occurs.

- Unreachable Customer Service:

Online retailers are typically not known for their customer service. Phone numbers and emails should be listed prominently on every page. Responses to customer requests should be prompt and courteous.

For more help and advice Contact

Taryn lee Johnston

taryn@fcmmedia.co.uk

www.fcmmedia.co.uk

CPSIA information can be obtained at www.ICGtesting.com
Printed in the USA
BVOW08s1455100515

399741BV00011B/227/P

9 781494 282370

Bringing WATER to People

Katacha Díaz

Rigby

To my husband,
Dr. Vic C. Knauf,
and Keebu
with all my love

The author wishes to thank Professor L. Stephen Lansing and Mr. Jeff Cohen, who generously shared information. Thanks also to Mr. I. Nyoman Chatra, who served as a guide and interpreter in Bali.

© 1997 by Rigby,
a division of Reed Elsevier Inc.
1000 Hart Rd.
Barrington, IL 60010-2627

All rights reserved. No part of this publication may be reproduced or transmitted in any form or by any means, electronic or mechanical, including photocopying, recording, taping, or any information storage and retrieval system, without permission in writing from the publisher.

04 03 02 01
10 9 8 7 6 5

Printed in Singapore
ISBN 0-7635-3178-2

Photo Credits

front cover background California Department of Water Resources
front cover inset Christopher Bissell/Tony Stone
back cover Katacha Díaz
2–3, 10–11, 18–19, 24–25, 31–32 background Meighan Depke
4–5 background Arnulf Husmo/Tony Stone
4 inset H. Richard Johnston/Tony Stone
5 inset Christopher Bissell/Tony Stone
6 Bob Thomas/Tony Stone
7 top Richard H. Smith/Tony Stone
7 bottom Keith Wood/Tony Stone
8–9 Yann Layma/Tony Stone
11 top Charles A. Mauzy/Tony Stone
11 bottom Peter Pearson/Tony Stone
12–14 California Department of Water Resources
15 Sharon Hoogstraten
16 R. Ravenstine
17 H. Richard Johnston/Tony Stone
19 top Nicholas DeVore/Tony Stone
19 bottom L. Stephen Lansing
20 Denis Waugh/Tony Stone
21 Katacha Díaz
22 L. Stephen Lansing
23 Katacha Díaz
25 top Michael Scott/Tony Stone
25 bottom Katacha Díaz
26–27 Katacha Díaz
28 David Tejada/Tony Stone
29 David C. Houston
30 left California Department of Water Resources
30 middle Denis Waugh/Tony Stone
30 right Michael Scott/Tony Stone